Christmas Dreams
A Cantata

By Joseph M. Martin and Heather Sorenson
Orchestrations by Brant Adams and Stan Pethel

① This symbol indicates a track number on the StudioTrax CD or SplitTrax CD.

Duration: ca. 56 Minutes

ISBN 9-781-5400-2712-2

Exclusively Distributed By

7777 W. BLUEMOUND RD. P.O. BOX 13819 MILWAUKEE, WI 53213

Visit Hal Leonard Online at
www.halleonard.com

Visit Shawnee Press Online at
www.shawneepress.com

Contact Us:
Hal Leonard
7777 West Bluemound Road
Milwaukee, WI 53213
Email: info@halleonard.com

In Europe contact:
Hal Leonard Europe Limited
Distribution Centre, Newmarket Road
Bury St Edmunds, Suffolk, IP33 3YB
Email: info@halleonardeurope.com

In Australia contact:
Hal Leonard Australia Pty. Ltd.
4 Lentara Court
Cheltenham, Victoria, 3192 Australia
Email: info@halleonard.com.au

FOREWORD

Throughout time, God has spoken to His people in dreams and visions. In the peacefulness of sleep and the serenity of contemplation, God speaks hope into longing hearts. Through the ancient prophets and devoted visionaries, He reveals the great designs of His creative purpose.

It is good and right that, in this wondrous season, we gather to remember, to reflect, to renew.

Let us quiet our hearts and listen.

Let us clear our minds and learn.

Let us calm our spirits and live.

Tonight, in the still, sacred places of our worship, in the fragile yearnings of our broken dreams, may we seek and discover the grace that changes everything.

Joseph M. Martin

CHRISTMAS DREAMS OVERTURE

Music by
HEATHER SORENSON (ASCAP)

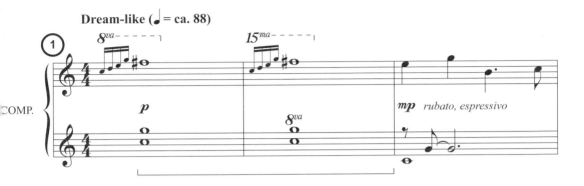

Slightly faster (♩ = ca. 100)

* Tune: MENDELSSOHN, Felix Mendelssohn, 1809-1847

CHRISTMAS DREAMS - SA

Broadly, sweeping (♩ = ca. 88)

Playfully (♩ = ca. 112)

Like the beginning ($\boldsymbol{\downarrow}$ = ca. 88)

* Tune: GLORIA, Traditional French Carol
** Tune: STILLE NACHT, Franz Grüber, 1787-1863

CHRISTMAS DREAMS - SA

NARRATION:
Throughout time, God has spoken to His people in dreams and visions. In the peacefulness of sleep and the serenity of contemplation, God speaks hope into longing hearts. Through the ancient prophets and devoted visionaries, He reveals the great designs of His creative purpose.

It is good and right, that in this wondrous season, we gather to remember, to reflect, to renew.

Let us quiet our hearts and listen.

Let us clear our minds and learn.

Let us calm our spirits and live.

Tonight, in the still, sacred places of our worship, in the fragile yearnings of our broken dreams, may we seek and discover the grace that changes everything.

SCRIPTURE:
For to us a Child is born, to us a Son is given, and the government will be on His shoulders. And He will be called Wonderful Counselor, Mighty God, Everlasting Father, Prince of Peace. *(Isaiah 9:6 NIV)*

ADVENT DREAMS

Words by
JOSEPH M. MARTIN (BMI)

Musi
HEATHER SORENSON (ASC
Incorporating Tu
SUSSEX CAR
Traditional Eng
GESÙ BAMBI
by PIETRO ALESSANDRO YON (1886-1

With joyful anticipation (♩. = ca. 66)

ACCOMP.

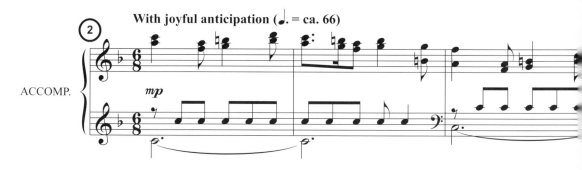

CHRISTMAS DREAMS - SA

dwell - ing place, and let the heal - ing start._____ Oh,

come_____ to us,_____ Em - man - u - el. We

lift our dreams to You._____ Our

hopes, _____ our prayers, each need, each

care. _____ Your word is ev - er

true. _____ Your word is ev - er

true.

God, who placed the hope___ of peace in ev - 'ry hu - man

dream,___

come and make our strug - gles cease, and

ny; a word of truth, a song of life, a

from the skies to teach us har - mo - ny; a

teach us har - mo - ny; a word of truth, a

sa - cred sym - pho - ny. Oh,

word of truth, a song of life, a sa - cred sym - pho - ny. Oh,

song of life, a sa - cred sym - pho - ny. Oh,

God of won-ders, hear our plea. De-scend to us to-day. O

come, and set Your peo-ple free, and take our sins a-

way. Oh, come, Thou long ex-pect-ed One. We

long to be___ re - stored.___

long to be___ re - stored, to be re - stored.

You are heav - en's Ho - ly One, our Dream, our

Hope, our Lord.___ Oh, come___ to

us, _____ Em - man - u - el. Re - store, and

make us new. _____ Our joy, _____ ou

fears, each pain, each tear, _____

NARRATION:
In the heart of God's people, there was a deep longing for reconciliation. The nation yearned for a Redeemer, a great Messiah who would return and re-establish the temple, and recreate a kingdom of peace.

During those dark days of waiting, the prophets of God offered words of challenge and encouragement. Daniel saw a new hope for the nation. Isaiah foresaw a new peace, founded in justice and truth. Hosea spoke of divine love and unending grace; and Zechariah proclaimed a day of joy and spiritual victory. God heard the prayers of His people, and in the fullness of time, the dream for a new covenant would be a reality.

SCRIPTURE:
"Behold, days are coming," declares the Lord, "when I will make a new covenant with the house of Israel and with the house of Judah, not like the covenant which I made with their fathers in the day I took them by the hand to bring them out of the land of Egypt. But this is the covenant which I will make with the house of Israel after those days," declares the LORD, "I will put My law within them and on their heart I will write it; and I will be their God, and they shall be My people." *(Jeremiah 31:31-33 Adapted)*

THE PROMISE AND THE PRAYER

ls by
EPH M. MARTIN (BMI)

Music by
HEATHER SORENSON (ASCAP)
Incorporating **CAROL OF THE BIRDS**
Traditional Catalonian Melody

Child Narrator:
Lord, speak to us in promises,
we bring our hopes to You.

Imperfect prayers are all we have; we long to be renewed.

Our fragile faith is reaching into the silent night.

We cling to Your assurance, Your covenant of light.

TENOR / BASS

Hear the long - ing of our hearts: "Lord, re - store our

CHRISTMAS DREAMS - SATB

man - u - el."

man - u - el.____ Come, Em - man - u - el."

man - u - el. Come, Em - man - u - el."

TENOR / BASS (11) [39] *mp* unis.

Hear   the long-ing

of   our hearts: "Lord, re - store our   hope."____

28

30

NARRATION:

The ancient prophets also foresaw the coming of a new day of truth and justice. In dreams, visions, and even angelic visitations, these faithful servants gave witness to the promises of God, and called the people to repent and prepare. They stirred the hearts of the people and gave them a hope that, one day, God would send a Redeemer. With bold exclamations, the prophets called the children of God from their dreams and into action.

SCRIPTURE:

"Awake, awake, put on your strength, O Zion. Jerusalem, put on your beautiful garments. Arise, shine; for your light has come, and the glory of the Lord has risen upon you. Now is the hour for you to wake from your sleep. Salvation is near!"

(Isaiah 52:1 NRSV, Isaiah 60:1 NRSV, Romans 13:11 Adapted)

A NEW MORNING OF PROMISE

Words and Music by
JOSEPH M. MARTIN (BMI)
Incorporating tune:
MORNING SONG
Traditional American Melody
Kentucky Harmony, 1813, alt.

Dream-ers a-wake! The dawn is near.

A - rise and face the day!

CHRISTMAS DREAMS - SATB

Lilting, lively (♩. = ca. 66)

SOPRANO

16

* *mf* unis.

ALTO

TENOR

mf unis.

The

BASS

peo - ple who—— in dark - ness walked will see a won - drous

light; for morning gilds the sky with gold, and

shines away the night. The morning gilds the

sky with gold, and shines away the night.

now,___ the time___ is draw - ing near, and hearts are filled___ wi

hope. Ve - ni, ve - ni.

Come,___ O come, Em - man - u - el. Ve - ni,

claim to the world a joy - ful song, the com - ing of___ the

Lord. Ve - ni,

ve - ni. Come,___ O come, Em - man - u - el.

NARRATION:

Zechariah and his wife Elizabeth were righteous persons. They had no children and were well past child bearing years when Zechariah was visited by the angel Gabriel. Gabriel told Zechariah that he would have a son who would be a forerunner of the Messiah. He was told to consecrate his son and name him John. This declaration was beyond Zechariah's wildest dreams! Amazed and unable to accept this miraculous news, he initially doubted the angel and was rendered mute until the baby was born. After nine months of silence and reflection, Zechariah was released from his silence and he immediately began singing praise to the Lord. It was clear that Jesus, the chosen One, was coming soon, and that John was to go before Him.

SCRIPTURE:

Praise be to the Lord, the God of Israel, because He has come to His people and redeemed them...And you, John, will be called a prophet of the Most High; for you will go on before the Lord to prepare the way for Him.
(Luke 1:68, 76 NIV)

ZECHARIAH'S SONG

Words by
JOSEPH M. MARTIN (BMI)

Based on t[...]
TEMPUS ADEST FLORID[...]
and **BRANLE DE L'OFFIC[...]**
Arrange[...]
JOSEPH M. MA[...]

* Tune: TEMPUS ADEST FLORIDUM, *Piae Cantiones,* 1582

You will call the ba - by John. He will know God

He will go be - fore the Lord, pre - par - ing for the

fa - vor!

Sav - ior. In the de - sert, he will preach; a voice of truth an

pow - er. Wake, rise up, pre - pare the way. This could be the

ve - ry hour!

Let your__ si - lence__ turn to song;

Al - le - lu - ia,

48

Re - joice, and lift your mu - sic fill the earth with sing - ing. Lift your mu - sic

fill the earth with sing - ing. Lift mu - sic

unis.

loud and strong. Won - ders are be - gin - ning.

loud and strong.

Sing praise to God, and be not si - lent!

f

Sing praise to God, and be not si - lent!_____

SOPRANO DESCANT

Al - le - lu - ia! Al - le - lu - ia!_____

Bless - ed be the Lord our God! Praise and ex - al - ta - tion!_____

CHRISTMAS DREAMS - SATB

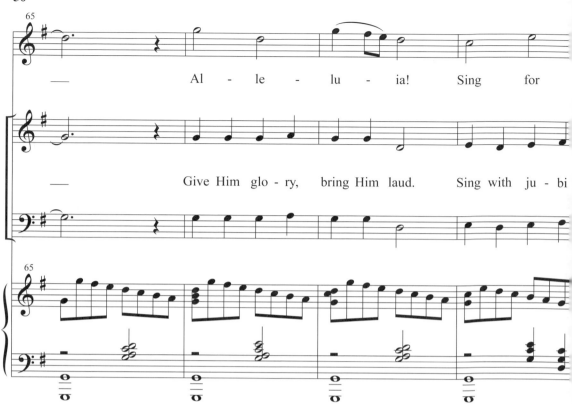

Al - le - lu - ia! Sing for

Give Him glo - ry, bring Him laud. Sing with ju - bi

joy!_____

la - tion!_____ Sound the trum-pet! Strike the drum!

(descant t

Shout with ex-pec - ta - tion! Soon the Morn-ing Star_will_come!

Join the cel - e - bra - tion!_____

with great rejoicing

Glo - ri - a! Glo - ri -
Glo - ri - a! Glo - ri -

Glo - ri - a!_____ Glo - ri -

with great rejoicing

Tune: BRANLE DE L'OFFICIEL, Thoinot Arbeau, 1520-1595   CHRISTMAS DREAMS - SATB

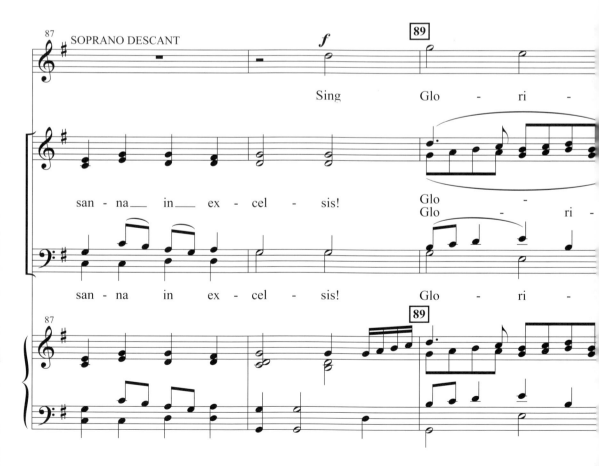

cel - sis!   Ho - san - na___

cel - sis!   Ho - san - na___

cel - sis!

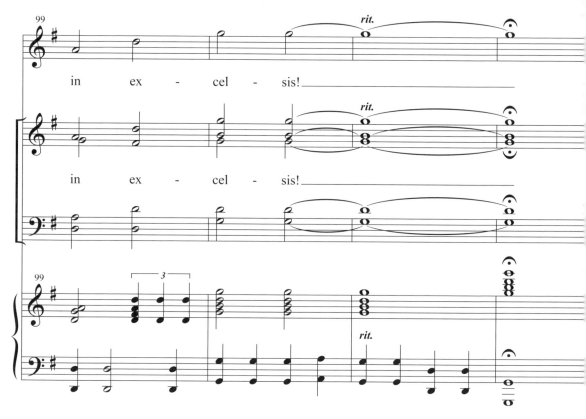

in   ex - cel - sis!_____

in   ex - cel - sis!_____

NARRATION:

Zechariah's wife Elizabeth had a cousin who was a young peasant girl from the small village called Nazareth. The girl's name was Mary, and she had been chosen by God to be the mother of Jesus who was the Messiah. In the sixth month, the angel Gabriel visited Mary and announced to her the miracle that was soon to happen in her life. Amazed and troubled at the angel's proclamation, she listened devotedly as Gabriel spoke:

SCRIPTURE:

"Do not be afraid, Mary; for you have found favor with God. And behold, you will concieve in your womb and bear a Son, and you shall call His name Jesus. He will be great and will be called the Son of the Most High. And the Lord God will give to Him the throne of His father David, and He will reign over the house of Jacob forever, and of His Kingdon there will be no end."

(Luke 1:30-33 ESV)*

MARY'S DREAM

Words and Mus.
JOSEPH M. MARTIN (

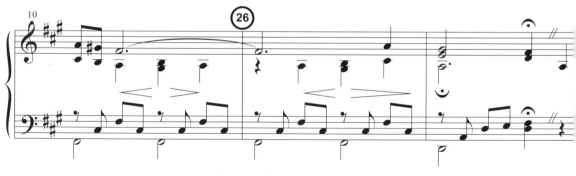

FEMALE SOLO

Long a-go,_____ gen-tle Ma-ry clings to hope and soft-ly prays._____ All a-lone,_____ star-ing at the night and dream-ing of the day_____ her lit-tle boy would come to

stay. She

dreams she hears Him cry - ing in the mid - dle of the night.

lightly agitated, with rubato

poco rit.

In her mind, she's hold - ing Him and sings a lull - a - by. She

a tempo

rit.

Oh, Je - sus,

Slowly, freely

how _ close I feel You to my heart,_____ my heart,___ my

heart,_____ my heart._____

NARRATION:
God chose Joseph, a just man, to be Mary's husband. When he discovered she was expecting a Child of the Holy Spirit, he pondered how to compassionately address this dilemma. Even as he considered this most unusual situation, an angel of the Lord appeared to him in a dream.

SCRIPTURE:
"Joseph, son of David, do not fear to take Mary as your wife, for that which is conceived in her is of the Holy Spirit; she will bear a Son, and you shall call His name Jesus, for He will save His people from their sins." When Joseph woke from sleep, he did as the angel of the Lord commanded him; he took Mary as his wife, and in the fullness of time she bore a Son; and he called His name Jesus. *(Matthew 1:20-25 Adapted)*

ALL THROUGH THE NIGHT

Traditional Welsh Folk Song

Additional Words and Arrangemen
HEATHER SORENSON (ASC
Quoting "Joy To the Wo

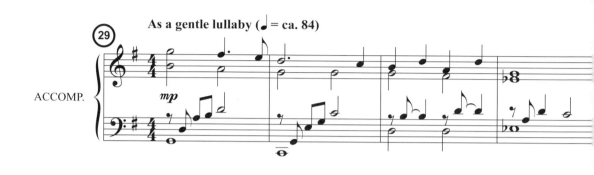

SOPRANO / ALTO

Sleep, my Child, and peace at-tend Thee, all through th

TENOR / BASS

CHRISTMAS DREAMS - SA

night.

Guard - ian an - gels God will send Thee,

all through the night.

19 *unis. (opt. Sopranos only)*

Soft, the drow - sy

hours are creep - ing; hill and dale in slum - ber sleep - ing.

CHRISTMAS DREAMS - SATB

Shad - ows beck - on, dark - ness threat-ens all through the night.

all through the night.

Lone - ly win - ter, bur - dens lin - ger all through the night.

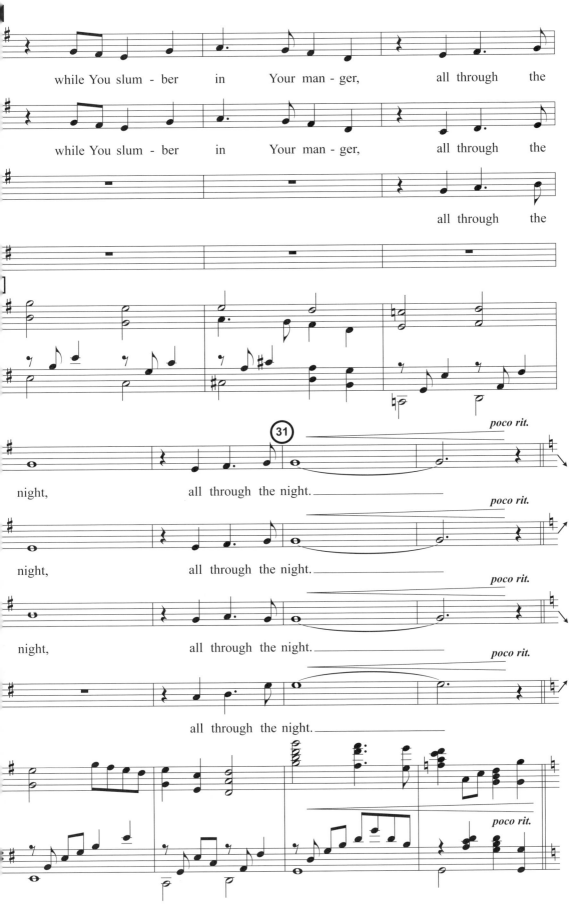

68

NARRATION:

It was a night of miracles and wonders when Jesus was born in Bethlehem. Mary and Joseph had been compelled to travel in order to register for the census ordered by the Roman authorities. When the time came for Mary to deliver her Baby, Joseph was unable to find accommodations for them. The city was overrun with pilgrims and the only place available was a rugged stable behind a traveler's lodge. In this humble shelter intended for animals, the Son of God was born into this world. Mary wrapped her newborn Son in swaddling clothes to keep Him warm through the night. Under His earthly parents' loving gaze, the infant Jesus rested and dreamed upon a bed of golden straw.

It would not be long before the news of Jesus' birth would be made known. Once again, angels were entrusted to deliver the important declaration. Hear the words of scripture:

SCRIPTURE:

And there were shepherds living out in the fields nearby, keeping watch over their flocks at night. An angel of the Lord appeared to them, and the glory of the Lord shone around them, and they were terrified. But the angel said to them, "Do not be afraid. I bring you good news of great joy that will be for all the people. Today, in the town of David, a Savior has been born to you; He is Christ, the Lord. This will be a sign to you: You will find a Baby, wrapped in cloths, and lying in a manger."

Suddenly, a great company of the heavenly host appeared with the angel, praising God and saying, "Glory to God in the highest, and on earth peace to those on whom His favor rests." *(Luke 2:8-14 Adapted)*

HARK! THE HERALD ANGELS SING

Words by
CHARLES WESLEY (1707-1788)

Tune: **MENDELSSO**
by FELIX MENDELSSOHN (1809-
Arrange
HEATHER SORENSON (AS

Hark! the her - ald an - gels sing,

"Glo - ry___ to the new - born King!"___

rec - on - ciled!"

Joy - ful, all ye na - tions rise.

Join the tri - umph of the skies.

mf

With th'an-gel - ic host pro - claim,

mf unis.

mf

"Christ is born in Beth - le - hem!"

Hark! the her - ald an - gels sing,

"Glo - ry to the new - born King!"

off - spring of the vir - gin's womb.

Veiled in flesh, the

Hail th'in - car - nate De - i - ty,

God - head see.

pleased as man with us to dwell, Je - sus, our Em -

Broadly (♩ = ca. 94)

ff SOP. 1 DESCANT

Hail the heav'n - born Prince of Peace! Hail the Son of

S. *ff* *unis.*
A.

Hail the heav'n - born Prince of Peace! Hail the Son of

T. *ff*
B.

Broadly (♩ = ca. 94)

ff

Right - eous - ness! Light and life to

Right - eous - ness! Light and life to

all He brings, ris'n with heal - ing in His

all He brings, ___ ris'n with heal - ing in His

wings.

wings.

Glo - ri

Mild He lays His glo - ry by, ___

a. Born to raise us

born that we no more may die. Born to raise us

from the earth, born to give sec - ond birth.

from the earth, born to give us sec - ond birth.

NARRATION:

Far from the village of Bethlehem, there were Magi who had been observing an unusually brilliant light that had appeared in the night skies. These star gazers were diligently seeking answers for this celestial phenomenon, and as they researched the ancient writings, they became convinced that the star was a sign from heaven. Trusting in their discovery, they formed a caravan and began to follow the star as it arched across the night skies. The scriptures tell us the thoughts and intentions of these dreamers of light:

SCRIPTURE:

Now after Jesus was born in Bethlehem of Judea in the days of Herod the king, behold, wise men from the east came to Jerusalem, saying, "Where is He who has been born King of the Jews? For we have seen His star in the East and have come to worship Him." *(Matthew 2:1-2 Adapted)*

THE MAGI'S EPIPHANY

rds by
EPH M. MARTIN (BMI)

Music by
HEATHER SORENSON (ASCAP)

I gaze in-to the mys-ter-y. I search its vast ex-

CHRISTMAS DREAMS - SATB

panse. I see the spin-ni... pag - eant-ry of heav-en's cos - mic dance.

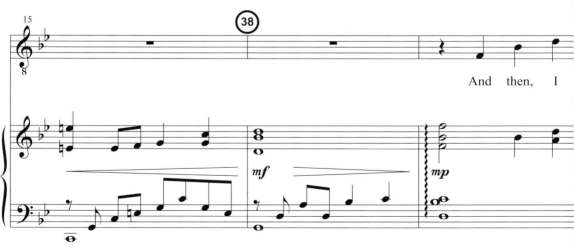

And then, I

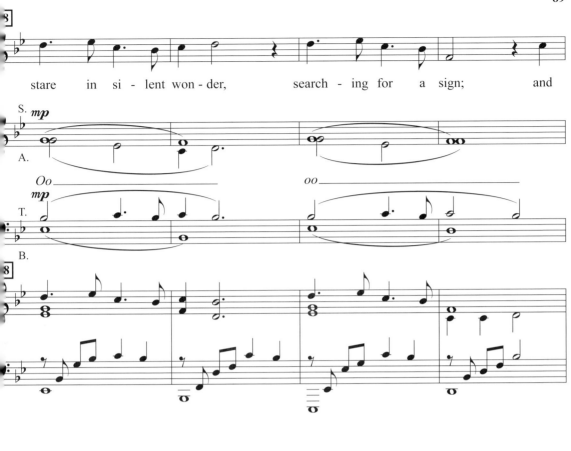

And then I see a star come ris - ing,

I see a star come ris - ing,

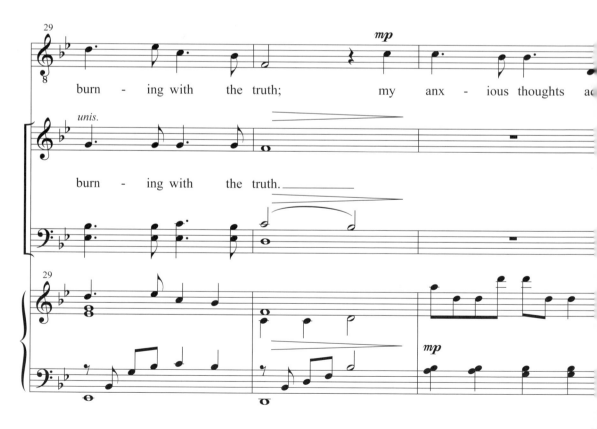

burn - ing with the truth; my anx - ious thoughts a⟨

burn - ing with the truth.

night. And then I fol - low where it takes me a - long a glo - rious way. It warms me and re-deems me, and melts my doubt a - way.

CHRISTMAS DREAMS - SATB

And then it leads me to a prom - ise, wher

life has found a place; where Light and Truth

wait - ing, where lies the Child of Grace.

Sometimes a light surprises a

seeker still today. A sacred star still

rises within the heart of faith.

Find and know. Leads them to a prom-ise,

know. And then it leads them to a prom-ise where

life found a place.

life has found a place; _____ where Light and Truth are wait-ing,

(end descant)

NARRATION:

In these sacred moments, we have joined our songs and spirits together to recall the birth of Jesus, the Messiah. We have heard the good news, and we are forever changed. We are now free to hope, believe, and become all that we were meant to be. Let us begin the true work of Christmas and dare to dream of a better world, a greater joy, a deeper faith.

Let us celebrate the graceful promises that are ours in Christ Jesus. Let us hold on to the divine hope that pursues us through every challenge of the heart and each illness of the mind and body. Let us rest secure in the grace that brings peace that is beyond all understanding.

SCRIPTURE:

For no eye has seen, no ear has heard, neither has it entered into the dreams of anyone, the wondrous things that God has prepared for those who love Him. *(1 Corinthians 2:9 Adapted)*

for Julien Wilbur Jamar

CHRISTMAS DREAMS

Words by
HEATHER SORENSON (ASCAP)
inspired and adapted from the anonymous poem
"Miracle Dreams"

Music
HEATHER SORENS...

On that Christ - mas night when mys - tic stars shone bright, a wist - ful blind man moved in sleep, an...

CHRISTMAS DREAMS - SA...

dreamed that he had sight. That night when shep - herds

TENOR / BASS

heard an an - gel *choir_____ near,

deaf man stirred in slum - ber's spell,

Oo_____ slum - ber's spell, and dreamed that he could

102

CHRISTMAS DREAMS - SA

dreamed that he was whole. He dreamed.
dreamed that he was whole. That

He dreamed.

night when o'er the Babe, young Ma - ry rose

lean, a loath - some lep - er smiled in sleep

night in man - ger lay the Child who came to save. A

man moved in the sleep of death, and dreamed there was no grave.___

Child of heal - ing, Child of hope, take the things that hurt us most, and

CHRISTMAS DREAMS - SATB

NARRATION:

And now, dreamers, rise and shine, for your light has come!

Hope now dazzles where once there was only darkness!

Love now sings where once there was only silence!

Joy now celebrates where once there was only sorrow!

Go now in peace, and take the dream of Christmas to all the world!

*dedicated in honor of Mary-Jo Yunaska Bedsworth on her 35th Anniversary as Director of Music
at Our Shepherd Lutheran Church, Severna Park, Maryland*

A GENTLE CHRISTMAS BLESSING

Words by
JOSEPH M. MARTIN (BMI)
Inspired by traditional Irish blessings

Music
JOSEPH M. MART
Incorporat
"Silent Night, Holy Nig

The cheer and good-will of friends to you,
Oo
and the
Oo
hope of a child - like heart to you.
17
mp
The hope of peace and grace to you, a safe and wel - come
mp
17
mp

place to you. The mu - sic of a thou - sand an - gels

be yours to-night, be yours in Christ. May love and joy a-bound i

all of life,___ God's love and joy sur - round your

Tune: STILLE NACHT, Franz Grüber, 1787-1863
Words: Joseph Mohr, 1792-1848; tr. John Freeman Young, 1820-1885

CHRISTMAS DREAMS - SATB

114

'round   yon   vir - gin   moth - er and   Child!

Ho - ly   In - fant so   ten - der and   mild,____

sleep____ in   heav - en - ly   peace,____

CHRISTMAS DREAMS - SA

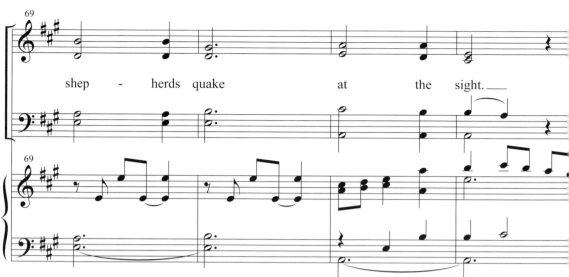

shep - herds quake at the sight.

Glo - ries stream from heav - en a - far.

Heav'n - ly hosts sing "Al - le-lu - ia,

Christ the Sav - ior is born,

Christ the Sav - ior is born."

87 Slower (♩ = ca. 70)